AP 19 '06	DATE DUE		

International Organizations

Greenpeace

Melanie Ostopowich

WEIGL PUBLISHERS INC.

Dedication

This series is dedicated to those people who help make their community, state, and world a better place. Volunteering is one way to become an active and responsible citizen. The thoughtfulness and hard work of volunteers is an inspiration to all. International Organizations is both an acknowledgment of and a tribute to volunteers.

Credits

Project Coordinator
Michael Lowry
Copy Editor
Jennifer Nault
Photo Researcher
Gayle Murdoff
Design and Layout
Warren Clark
Bryan Pezzi

Published by Weigl Publishers Inc.
123 South Broad Street, Box 227
Mankato, MN 56002
USA

Web site: www.weigl.com
Copyright ©2003 WEIGL PUBLISHERS INC.

Library of Congress Cataloging-in-Publication Data

Ostopowich, Melanie.
  Greenpeace / Melanie Ostopowich.
     p. cm. -- (International organizations)
Summary: Highlights the history, membership, mission, goals, and achievements of Greenpeace. Includes human interest stories, maps, timelines, Web sites, and suggestions for further reading.
Includes bibliographical references and index.
  ISBN 1-59036-020-6 (lib. bdg. : alk. paper)
  1. Greenpeace International--History--Juvenile literature. 2. Environmental protection--Juvenile literature. [1. Greenpeace International. 2. Environmental protection.] I. Title. II. Series.
  TD169 .O84 2002
  333.72'06'01--dc21
                                                        2002006562

Printed in Canada
1 2 3 4 5 6 7 8 9 0   06 05 04 03 02

Photo Credits

Every reasonable effort has been made to trace ownership and to obtain permission to reprint copyright material. The publishers would be pleased to have any errors or omissions brought to their attention so that they may be corrected in subsequent printings.

Cover: DigitalVision Ltd; **Bettmann/CORBIS/MAGMA:** pages 7, 11; **Corbis Corporation:** pages 12, 22 right; **Digital Stock Corporation:** page 13; **DigitalVision Ltd:** pages 3, 22 left, 27; ©**Greenpeace/Ferrero:** page 21 top; ©**Greenpeace/Keziere:** page 20; ©**Greenpeace/Morgan:** pages 5, 15; ©**Greenpeace/Kiryu:** page 23; ©**Greenpeace/Moore:** page 25; ©**Greenpeace/Periera:** page 21 bottom; ©**Greenpeace/Sims:** page 9; **Al Harvey:** page 6.

Text Credits

Greenpeace (http://www.greenpeace.org): quotations on pages 4, 6, 7, 8, 10, 18, 24, 27.

Contents

What is Greenpeace?

Greenpeace is an international environmental organization that works to protect the earth's natural resources and the many types of plant and animal life that live on earth.

Originally formed to protest nuclear testing in Alaska, Greenpeace has become a worldwide organization with nearly forty offices in more than thirty countries. Today, Greenpeace works to protect **biodiversity**, to prevent pollution of the earth's land and water, to achieve global nuclear disarmament, and to promote world peace.

Since its humble beginnings, Greenpeace has gained worldwide attention and support with daring and often dangerous feats. The world watched as Greenpeace members in rubber rafts tried to prevent whaling expeditions by positioning their rafts between the whales and the hunters' harpoons.

Greenpeace uses several methods when conducting campaigns, including scientific research, political **lobbying**, public education, and **direct action**.

Independent of governments, political parties, and industry, Greenpeace is largely supported by its more than 3 million members and voluntary funding.

"It is an incredible feeling when you believe in something so much and do everything in your power to make it happen, and then it happens. All that pushing, hard work and determination has paid off."
Jon Castle, Greenpeace Captain

In 1998, Greenpeace flew a balloon over the Taj Mahal to protest nuclear testing in India.

Quick Fact
Greenpeace owns a fleet of six ships, one helicopter, one bus, and one hot air balloon.

Just the Facts

Founded: In 1971, Greenpeace was formed in Vancouver, British Columbia, Canada to oppose nuclear testing in Alaska.

Founders: Jim Bohlen, Paul Cote, and Irving Stowe founded Greenpeace.

Mission: To protect biodiversity in all its forms; to prevent pollution of the earth's oceans, land, air, and fresh water; to end all nuclear threats; and to promote peace, global disarmament, and nonviolence.

Number of member organizations: Thirty-nine

Scope of work: Greenpeace works to protect the environment in countries all over the world, and is credited with prompting more than twenty-six international **treaties**.

An Organization is Born

The story of Greenpeace began in 1971, in Vancouver, British Columbia, Canada. Three friends, Jim Bohlen, Paul Cote, and Irving Stowe, were all members of a small group called the Don't Make a Wave Committee. The group was opposed to nuclear weapons testing by the U.S. military in Amchitka, a small island off the west coast of Alaska.

They believed they could make a difference by using the **Quaker** tradition of "bearing witness," which means protesting an injustice by simply being there to observe it. They attempted to take a boat to one of the nuclear testing sites in Alaska in hopes of stopping the blast.

It was during a planning meeting of the Don't Make a Wave Committee that Greenpeace was born. The small group decided to rename itself Greenpeace to reflect their goal of creating a "green" and peaceful world.

While the group failed to stop the nuclear blast, the voyage itself was a great success. The modern-day "David and Goliath" story received attention from all over the world. As the voyage advanced, Greenpeace gained support from across the globe.

Even though the nuclear test went ahead, public opposition became so powerful that U.S. President Richard Nixon had to cancel the nuclear testing the following year. The Greenpeace movement had begun.

> "Greenpeace has played a central role in changing the course of world events ... during the past three decades."
>
> Chris Rose, Greenpeace UK

Greenpeace was formed in the city of Vancouver, which is located on the western coast of Canada. Today, nearly 2 million people live in and around Vancouver.

PROFILES

Jim Bohlen

Born in New York, Jim Bohlen was a deep-sea diver and radar operator in the United States Navy in World War II. During the war, Bohlen was involved in the design of a missile rocket motor system. It was later used as a component for the very same nuclear weapons that Greenpeace condemned.

The power and capacity for destruction of nuclear weapons disturbed Bohlen. After the Cuban missile crisis of 1962, he became more dissatisfied with government policies. The missile crisis was a major confrontation between the United States and the former Soviet Union, and is regarded by many as the world's closest encounter with nuclear war.

Bohlen was against U.S. involvement in the Vietnam War. Once his stepson was old enough to be drafted, he moved his family to British Columbia, where they made their home on an island north of Vancouver.

Irving Stowe

Irving Stowe was a Yale-educated lawyer from New England. In 1961, he moved

J. Bohlen   J. Cormack (skipper)   I. Stowe   P. Cote

"I was on the first Greenpeace voyage in 1971 ... I see the spirit of that original voyage in today's Greenpeace. We set out to make waves and we are succeeding."
Jim Bohlen

his family to New Zealand. He left the United States because he, too, feared a nuclear war. In 1966, the family moved to Vancouver where Stowe became involved with *The Georgia Straight*, a newspaper with antiwar beliefs.

It was Stowe who introduced Bohlen to the Quaker religion. Quakers believe in a form of protest known as "bearing witness." This later became a guiding principle for Greenpeace.

Paul Cote

Paul Cote, a young Canadian lawyer, had just completed university when he met Jim Bohlen and Irving Stowe. He met them at a protest at a United States/Canadian border crossing. The protest was aimed at the U.S. Atomic Energy Commission, which was running underground nuclear weapons tests on a small island near Alaska called Amchitka.

The Mission

The Greenpeace movement was born in the 1970s. It was in this decade that the environmental movement really began to gain strength, as well as the hope for global peace. During this period, the threat of nuclear war was great and many protest groups were formed.

While Greenpeace itself began for these same reasons, it stands for much more today. Greenpeace has become a global organization for people who wish to challenge those who damage and pollute the planet.

Greenpeace is made up of dedicated people who wish to make a difference in the world. The organization operates on several levels. Some methods are very public and some are behind-the-scenes. Greenpeace conducts scientific research, communicates with the public and the media, and carries out direct action, such as protesting. Greenpeace also organizes **boycotts** of companies believed to be harming the planet. It also communicates directly with the government over such issues as environmental policy.

Greenpeace is an independent, nonprofit organization that uses nonviolent, creative methods. It seeks to expose global environmental problems and their causes. The organization researches solutions and alternatives. Greenpeace's goal is to protect the earth's ability to nurture life in all its diversity.

> "Since its inception in 1971, Greenpeace has worked to end the threat of nuclear war."
> Greenpeace USA

Quick Fact •

While it has only 4 percent of the world's population, the United States emits more greenhouse gases than any other nation. The United States is responsible for 22 percent of global emissions of greenhouse gases.

Greenpeace works for:

- the protection of the oceans and ancient forests

- the phasing-out of fossil fuels and the promotion of **renewable** energy sources in order to stop climate change

- the elimination of toxic chemicals

- the continued use of natural products and the halting of the release of genetically modified organisms (GMOs) into nature

- nuclear disarmament and an end to nuclear contamination

In 1995, Greenpeace occupied the abandoned oil storage facility, the Brent Spar, to prevent it from being dumped into the North Sea. The Brent Spar was later dismantled in Norway following a public outcry.

Key Issues

Greenpeace strives to protect the environment and preserve the world we live in for the enjoyment of future generations. The environment is facing a wide range of threats across the globe. Greenpeace has identified certain key issues that put stress on our environment.

Global Warming

The burning of fossil fuels, such as oil, coal, and gas, is a contributing factor to **global warming**. When fossil fuels are burned, carbon dioxide is released into the **atmosphere**, where it remains, causing a "greenhouse effect." Much like a greenhouse for plants, the air close to the earth becomes warmer.

Quick Fact

The first three months of 2002 were the warmest in recorded history, and probably the warmest in the last 1,000 years.

The effects of temperature changes on the environment can be devastating. Warmer temperatures at the earth's poles have already been linked to the melting of the polar ice caps. This could result in higher sea levels, unstable weather patterns, and the **extinction** of some plant and animal species.

Greenpeace has long been involved in heightening awareness about global warming, and has campaigned to reduce the human impact on global warming. Greenpeace advocates the use of environmentally friendly energy sources, such as solar and wind power, in place of fossil fuels. The organization asks that industries take more responsibility for their actions, and that the government supports the use of clean forms of energy.

Forests

The importance of forests to the earth is clear. It is estimated that the ancient forests are home to 80 percent of the world's land-based plant and animal species. Forests also work to recycle the carbon dioxide that is in the atmosphere. The leaves on the trees absorb carbon dioxide and release oxygen.

Despite the benefits of the earth's forests, more than 80 percent of the world's ancient forests have been destroyed or damaged by logging, or cleared for farming.

To help protect the earth's remaining forests, Greenpeace launched the Kids for Forests Web site, which provides information about forests and the animals living in them.

CASE STUDY
The Nuclear Weapons Testing Campaign

In 1983, Greenpeace actively campaigned against the testing of nuclear weapons. It wanted the U.S., Britain, and the former Soviet Union to sign a nuclear test ban treaty.

Greenpeace protesters traveled to the Nevada test site, where the United States had conducted more than 800 nuclear tests. The protesters managed to hide from officials, who searched for them for four days. The officials were forced to postpone the nuclear test.

In Germany, another bold protest took place on August 28, 1983. Greenpeace **activists** flew a hot air balloon over the Berlin Wall into the former East Germany. The protesters carried signs calling for peace and disarmament. After landing, the protesters were arrested.

The campaign came to an end thirteen years later. A treaty banning all nuclear testing was signed in 1996.

"[Not achieving a nuclear test ban] would have to be classed as the greatest disappointment of any administration, of any decade, of any time and of any party."
President Dwight D. Eisenhower, 1961

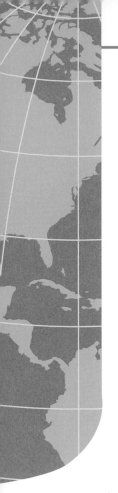

Genetic Engineering

Genetically modified organisms (GMOs) can be found in thousands of products on supermarket shelves across the country. These organisms can be plant, animal, or bacterial, and have all had their **genes** altered in some way.

Farmers have been selectively breeding plants and animals for thousands of years. However, recent scientific advances have made it possible to combine genes of species that cannot breed naturally. For example, genes from a fish have been inserted into strawberries and tomatoes to prevent frost damage. Chemicals can also be inserted into food crops to protect them from diseases, insects, and pesticides. Greenpeace has published the *True Food Shopping List: How to Avoid Genetically Altered Foods*, to aid people who wish to avoid these foods.

Most of the genetically engineered foods found in grocery stores are not required to be labeled.

Nuclear Disarmament

Since 1971, when a small group of activists sailed to Alaska to protest nuclear testing, Greenpeace has been campaigning against nuclear technologies.

Many nations now have the capability to construct nuclear bombs. For this reason, Greenpeace believes that nuclear disarmament should be a top international priority. In addition, it believes that the trade in nuclear materials should stop and that nuclear power be replaced with renewable energy sources.

CASE STUDY
The Save the Whales Campaign

The Save the Whales campaign, which is perhaps the most well-known Greenpeace campaign, did not begin until 1975. Due to modern technology, the practice of whaling was threatening to bring many whale species to the brink of extinction. This was happening despite the fact that the International Whaling Commission (IWC) had been formed in 1946 to prevent that very possibility.

The Greenpeace Save the Whales campaign, founded by Robert Hunter and Paul Spong, attempted to stop the practice of commercial whaling. Greenpeace knew that it needed to gain public support by highlighting the issues. It also knew that the best way to raise public awareness was to put itself in the middle of the action. Greenpeace hoped this would also stop the hunt.

The Greenpeace activists tracked and located a Russian whaling fleet. Using speedboats, they raced to place themselves between the hunters and their target, a **pod** of ten sperm whales. Despite the danger to the Greenpeace protesters, a harpoon was thrown, killing a nearby female sperm whale.

After eighty-four days of protest, eight of the ten sperm whales had been saved. The television and newspaper coverage of the protest and hunt brought the issue of commercial whaling to people around the world.

Public pressure to end commercial whaling increased year after year. In 1982, the IWC voted to end the practice. However, in recent years, Norway has defied the ban, and Japan has continued whaling for scientific study.

In 1994, another victory was added to the whale campaign. The IWC created the Southern Ocean Whale Sanctuary covering 11 million square miles and overlapping another protected area, the Indian Ocean Sanctuary.

Oceans

Oceans play a vital role in supporting biodiversity and controlling climate and weather patterns. They also provide a livelihood for people in coastal regions throughout the world.

Greenpeace has several key concerns involving oceans. These include over-fishing, poor fishing practices, and commercial whaling. Greenpeace is currently campaigning to ban the use of factory trawlers. Factory trawlers are large floating factories, which often use **drift nets** measuring up to four football fields in length. The problem with nets this size is that they often trap a large amount of unwanted fish and other marine life known as "bycatch." This bycatch usually dies and is dumped back into the ocean.

Greenpeace has developed a document entitled *Principles for Ecologically Responsible Fisheries*, which provides guidelines for better fishing methods. The organization is urging congress, the National Marine Fish Service, and the fishing industry to adopt these methods. In 1998, Greenpeace began the Save Our Seas bus tour, which travels across the United States, educating the public along the way.

Toxins

The worst toxins in our environment today are known as POPs, or persistent organic pollutants. POPs, such as the pesticide DDT, are highly poisonous in very small amounts and can remain in the environment for a long time. POPs occur all over the world; they can be found in the air we breathe, the water we drink, and the food we eat.

These toxins can be stored in living tissue, passing from mother to child and resulting in a variety of health problems, including cancer.

Greenpeace works to eliminate POPs from our environment by promoting cleaner industrial processes. This includes using renewable, non-hazardous materials, and more efficient energy resources.

Quick Fact ·······································

Many scientists estimate that sea levels will rise by 10 to 34 inches over the next eighty years as a result of global warming.

CASE STUDY
The Antarctica Campaign

In 1985, Antarctica, the most untouched continent in the world, became the subject of a Greenpeace campaign.

In the early 1980s, Antarctica came under the threat of commercial development. Many countries had expressed the desire to see it turned into a World Park. However, an existing treaty protecting the continent was close to ending. A wealth of oil and mineral deposits were thought to be under the ice. It was becoming more likely that Antarctica would be commercially developed after the treaty ended.

Greenpeace decided that the best way to campaign for Antarctica to be designated a World Park was to set up a permanent base on the continent. In 1986, after several failed attempts, a team of four Greenpeace activists made it to the icy continent. They planned to spend the entire winter in Antarctica.

Three weeks later, the World Park Base was created.

In keeping with Greenpeace's environmentally friendly mission, every effort was made to minimize human impact. The permanent base was in place for four years, from 1987 to 1991.

Eventually, the original treaty signers decided to make Antarctica a World Park. In 1991, the signatories of the 1958 Antarctica Treaty agreed to adopt a new Environmental Protocol. This included a fifty-year minimum ban on all mining.

"Outside my window the sea ice is in full melt and the stretches of open water are growing before our eyes. In the Cape Evans area more than twenty Weddell seals are basking ashore and the Skua chicks are growing."
Phil Doherty, Greenpeace Volunteer at the World Park Base, 1990

Around the World

Since Greenpeace was formed in Vancouver, British Columbia, Canada, in 1971, offices have opened in many other countries. The mission remains the same the world over—to protect the environment, promote peace, and ensure a healthy planet for future generations to enjoy.

Countries with Greenpeace offices are colored in yellow on this map. Some countries have more than one office.

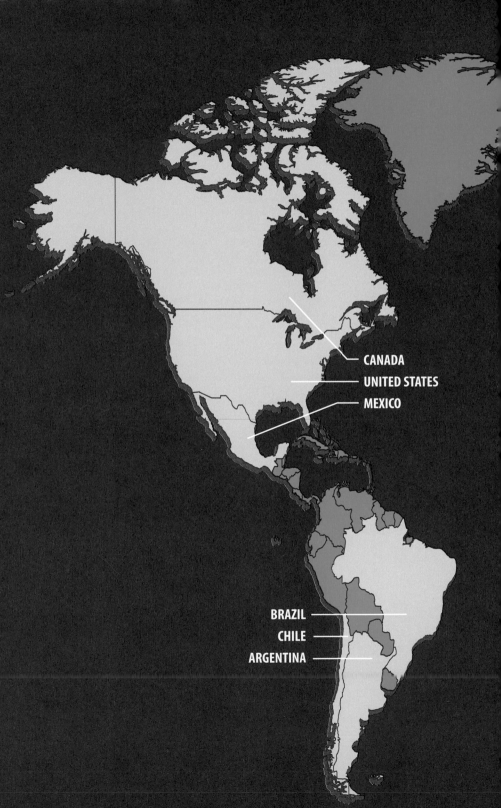

CANADA

UNITED STATES

MEXICO

BRAZIL

CHILE

ARGENTINA

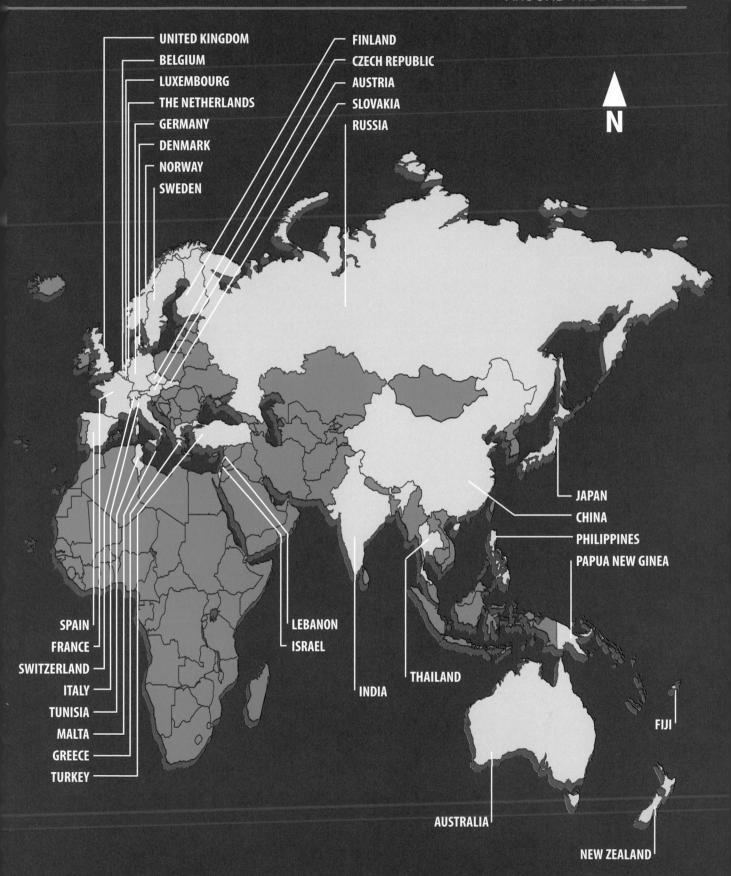

UNITED KINGDOM

BELGIUM

LUXEMBOURG

THE NETHERLANDS

GERMANY

DENMARK

NORWAY

SWEDEN

FINLAND

CZECH REPUBLIC

AUSTRIA

SLOVAKIA

RUSSIA

N

JAPAN

CHINA

PHILIPPINES

PAPUA NEW GINEA

SPAIN

FRANCE

SWITZERLAND

ITALY

TUNISIA

MALTA

GREECE

TURKEY

LEBANON

ISRAEL

THAILAND

INDIA

FIJI

AUSTRALIA

NEW ZEALAND

U.S. Operations

Greenpeace opened offices in San Francisco, California and Portland, Oregon in 1975. Today, Greenpeace has more than 250,000 members in the United States.

"It's something you do because you care ... either we win and we still have an environment, or we don't—and there's nothing to discuss."

Tami Edwards, Greenpeace Member

Environmental problems occur all over the world, regardless of how economically developed a country may be. In fact, it is often the large, wealthy countries that have the most negative impact on the environment.

Greenpeace is working on a variety of projects in the U.S., including the Clean Energy Now campaign, currently underway in California. Greenpeace, along with local groups, is working to reduce California's impact on the environment. Greenpeace hopes California will become the world's largest clean energy economy.

California has the fifth-largest economy in the world. However, it ranks globally as the sixth-largest greenhouse gas emitter. Greenpeace is working toward changing this statistic. In a victory for the campaign, San Francisco voted to approve funding for solar energy facilities.

In another ongoing campaign, Greenpeace is targeting the use of genetically modified organisms (GMOs) in foods. Greenpeace launched the True Food Network to educate the public about genetically engineered foods. This network provides information on how to avoid GMOs. It also identifies which food products contain them.

Greenpeace USA does not limit itself to campaigns within its national borders. It is involved with campaigns worldwide, including saving the earth's forests and protecting the oceans.

Quick Fact •

In 30 minutes, the surface of the earth receives enough energy from the Sun to power the entire planet for one year.

CASE STUDY
The Kyoto Protocol

In December 1997, a group of industrialized countries signed the Kyoto Protocol. This international treaty sets targets for reducing levels of pollution in an effort to slow down global warming. The United States signed the treaty, as well as Japan and the countries of the European Union. They agreed to reduce pollution from industry and gave themselves a deadline of September 2002 to meet their targets.

Since then, Greenpeace has actively campaigned to remind countries of their promise to the environment. Activists have come together to organize protests and demonstrations in cities such as Paris, France and Madrid, Spain. Their aim is to encourage world leaders to continue working toward the targets set in the Kyoto Protocol.

The United States produces more pollution than any other country. Although it has only 4 percent of the world's population, it creates a quarter of the total carbon dioxide released into the atmosphere every year. This gas contributes to global warming. However, in March 2001, President George W. Bush announced that the United States would not reach the targets set out in the Kyoto agreement.

Greenpeace is campaigning to pressure the president to fulfill his promises. In 2001, Greenpeace activists released a hot air balloon high above a glacier in Argentina. Written on the balloon were the words "Bush & Co. = Climate Disaster." Many people witnessed the huge balloon floating over the ice.

As part of its campaign, Greenpeace is also targeting major oil and gas companies, because carbon dioxide is created by burning fossil fuels such as oil and gas. Activists hang banners on buildings and bridges, shut down oil rigs, and demonstrate at oil company headquarters and even small gas stations.

Milestones

Greenpeace has been working to protect the environment by using non-violent, direct action throughout the world for more than thirty years. As Greenpeace has grown and developed, it has supported this direct action with political lobbying and scientific enquiry.

1971: The Maiden Voyage of Greenpeace

September 15, 1971, marks the first voyage of Greenpeace, when a group of twelve activists sail from Vancouver, British Columbia, Canada to the Aleutian Islands near Alaska. The crew sail aboard the *Phyllis Cormack*. They are protesting the testing of nuclear weapons at Amchitka.

1971

The Don't Make A Wave Committee changes its name to Greenpeace.

1972

Five months after the Greenpeace protest at Amchitka, Alaska, the United States announces an end to nuclear testing in the Aleutian Islands due to "political and other reasons."

1975

Greenpeace opens its first American offices in San Francisco, California and Portland, Oregon.

1975

Greenpeace begins the first of many ocean voyages to confront commercial whaling ships.

1978

With the aid of a grant from the World Wildlife Fund, Greenpeace buys its first ship, the *Rainbow Warrior*.

1981

In one of the first victories of Greenpeace's Save the Whales campaign, the International Whaling Commission bans the hunting of sperm whales.

1982

The International Whaling Commission votes to end all commercial whaling within three years. The only objections to this decision come from Japan, Norway, Peru, and the former Soviet Union.

1978: The Naming of the *Rainbow Warrior*

Inspired by a North American Cree legend, the Rainbow Warrior story predicts that when humans have destroyed the world through their greed, the Warriors of the Rainbow will arise to save it again. "When the world is sick and dying, the people will rise up like Warriors of the Rainbow ... "

To honor this legend, the boat is painted in rainbow patterns. A dove of peace carrying an olive branch is painted on the bow of the ship.

1985: The Rongelap Mission

On May 17, 1985, the *Rainbow Warrior* travels to the Marshall Islands in the Pacific to relocate the entire population of the island of Rongelap. Greenpeace had received a request for help from the Marshall Islands Parliament. The people of Rongelap had been exposed to radiation from U.S. nuclear testing in the area almost thirty years before. There are still many health problems, including birth defects and high incidences of cancer. Greenpeace agrees to relocate the entire population to the safer island of Mejato. The evacuation takes ten days and four trips between the two islands. Greenpeace relocates 300 islanders and more than 100 tons of building materials.

1986

Greenpeace activists set up a permanent base on Antarctica to protect it from development.

1987

Several years after Greenpeace's acid rain campaign, the United Nations enacts standards and guidelines in an attempt to stop the destruction of forests and the pollution of lakes.

1983

In a victory for the Greenpeace energy conservation campaign, the U.S. Congress suspends lease sales for offshore oil drilling off Cape Cod, northern California, and southwest Florida.

1984

On the anniversary of the Hiroshima bombing, Greenpeace protesters scale the scaffolding of the Statue of Liberty. The activists remain on the statue for five hours, calling for an end to nuclear testing.

1985

On July 10, while moored in Auckland harbor, New Zealand, the *Rainbow Warrior* is destroyed by a bomb planted by French secret service agents. Greenpeace photographer Fernando Pereira is killed in the explosion.

1987

Iceland announces an end to scientific whaling after being pressured by Greenpeace and the public.

1988

In a victory for the toxic waste campaign, sixty-five countries at the London Convention agree to halt the incineration of toxic waste at sea by the end of 1994.

1989

The United Nations General Assembly prohibits the expansion of drift-net activities. They are to be eliminated entirely by 1992.

1991

Antarctica is designated a World Park after nine years of campaigning.

1993

The United States stops nuclear weapons testing. Since the U.S. began testing nuclear weapons on July 16, 1945, they have conducted more than 1,000 tests throughout the world. This is the equivalent of one test every seventeen days.

1988: The Toxic Trade Campaign

Greenpeace launches the toxic trade campaign. A Philadelphia-based toxic ash export company is forced to retrieve a shipment of its waste from Guinea. The waste had been intended for Panama. It is turned away by the government and temporarily dumped in Guinea after the Panama government receives warnings from Greenpeace.

1994

The Southern Ocean Whale Sanctuary is established, protecting whales at risk of whaling activities.

1995

The United Nations agrees to a global fisheries treaty. It is the first of its kind.

1995

After a Greenpeace campaign and public pressure, the giant oil company, Shell, reverses its decision to dump an old oil storage facility, the Brent Spar, into the North Atlantic Ocean.

1995: The Washington Declaration

In a victory for the toxic trade campaign, international governments agree on the Washington Declaration. It calls for a global treaty to restrict production of persistent organic pollutants (POPs). Toxic substances, such as POPs, have been linked to a variety of health problems, including cancer.

1993: The London Convention

The final signing of the London Convention is completed. This occurs after a Greenpeace investigation uncovers the Russians dumping liquid radioactive waste into the Sea of Japan. The agreement permanently bans the dumping of radioactive waste at sea.

1999

Greenpeace reveals the presence of genetically engineered ingredients in some baby foods.

1999–2000

Home Depot and IKEA announce their commitments to stop selling wood products taken from environmentally sensitive areas.

2000

After the Greenpeace Atlantic Ocean Expedition, twenty-eight countries agree to ban the import of illegally caught tuna.

2001

After a Greenpeace campaign lasting ten years, more than ninety nations, including the United States, sign the first global treaty to stop the use of twelve of the most toxic chemicals.

1996

The five nuclear powers, China, France, Russia, Britain, and the U.S., sign the Comprehensive Nuclear Test Ban Treaty. The treaty must now be **ratified** by the member countries.

1997

Greenpeace receives an award for inventing the Greenfreeze, a refrigerator that does not contain **ozone**-damaging chemicals.

1998

Greenpeace and local activists prevent the building of a PVC plastic production facility in Convent, Louisiana. PVC is the most damaging plastic to public health and the environment.

Current Initiatives

Ancient Forests

Greenpeace has undertaken a global campaign to bring attention to the destruction of the world's remaining natural forests. These ancient forests are found all over the world and are home to countless plant, animal, and human populations. Their survival is dependent on the continued existence of these forests.

One part of the campaign is focused on saving the approximately 3.3 billion acres of ancient forest that remains undisturbed by large-scale industrial activities. The other part of the campaign was focused on the Ancient Forest Summit in the Netherlands. At this summit, the United Nations discussed an eight-year plan for the protection of our ancient forests.

Greenpeace sought commitments from the summit participants to:

- stop the further destruction of ancient forests through industrial activity until plans that address the environmental impact are in place.
- regulate the timber trade so that it complies with environmentally responsible policies.
- spend at least $15 billion each year on forest conservation and alternative economic development.

> "World governments must choose now to save or delete the world's remaining ancient forests."
>
> **Greenpeace International**

Quick Fact

More than eighty-seven cultural groups have disappeared in Brazil alone through the destruction of ancient forests. In the next ten to twenty years, the world will likely lose thousands of species of plants and animals as the result of deforestation.

CASE STUDY
The Seal Hunt Campaign

The commercial killing of the harp seal prompted Greenpeace to launch a campaign in 1976.

Every spring, Norway and Canada have carried out seal hunts on the eastern coast of Canada. Harp seal pups were killed by the thousands for their snow-white fur, which was then used for gloves, coats, and other luxury goods. Most furs were exported to Europe. Pups were clubbed on the head and stripped of their fur right on the ice.

Each year, from 1976 to 1984, Greenpeace activists traveled to Belle Isle, Newfoundland, where they protested against seal hunting. They placed themselves in front of seal ships to protect the seals from hunters. Another tactic Greenpeace members used was to paint the seal pups' fur with a harmless green dye, leaving the fur commercially worthless.

Soon, worldwide media attention made the seal hunt an international issue. In 1982, the European parliament passed a law against the import of harp- and hooded-seal pup skins. This destroyed the market for seal pup fur.

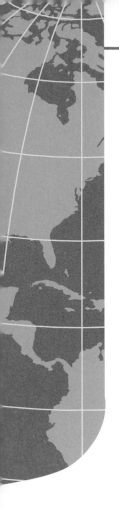

Stop Star Wars

Another Greenpeace campaign is the Stop Star Wars campaign. The current U.S. missile defense plan to set up land-, sea-, air- and space-based systems has been estimated to cost between $60 and $200 billion.

Greenpeace believes this plan defies everything it has worked for in the hopes of nuclear disarmament. The organization takes the following standpoints:

- Star Wars upsets the relationship between the United States and other nuclear states. It will compromise and block important arms control agreements.
- The U.S. government supports Star Wars as a necessary plan for national defense. However, other nations pose little to no nuclear threat to the United States. Most countries do not have the weapons needed to launch a successful nuclear attack against the United States.
- Greenpeace supports negotiation and diplomacy as the best course of action. It believes that acquiring more and more nuclear weapons will not make the nation more secure.
- Greenpeace continues to support worldwide nuclear disarmament.

If deforestation continues at current rates, the world's rainforests may completely disappear by 2030.

Quick Fact · · · · · · · · · · · · · · · · ·

Each Greenpeace national office functions with a board and voting members. Each office has its own independent structure, based on the needs and laws of the country. These offices are part of the international organization of Greenpeace but also maintain their own campaign priorities.

CASE STUDY
Into the Heart of the Amazon: The Greenpeace Deni Expedition

In 1999, Greenpeace began working with the Deni. They are a group of 600 people living in a remote area of the Amazon rainforest.

Greenpeace discovered that part of the area belonging to the Deni had been sold to a Malaysian logging company. Greenpeace traveled to the Amazon to tell the Deni. Although the area had been sold two years before, the Deni did not know about the deal. The Deni asked Greenpeace to help them fight for their right to the land.

A group of international Greenpeace volunteers went to the Amazon to live and work with the Deni for six months. Greenpeace helped them prepare to take back land that they felt was rightfully theirs.

By teaching the Deni how to use modern survey equipment and read maps, Greenpeace helped the group understand the idea of borders and how to mark the land.

"The Deni spent the day surveying and cutting their demarcation line, while we hauled water, cooked, and established radio communication with the main boat."
Bryan, Greenpeace volunteer
in the Amazon rainforest

Take Action!

If you would like to get involved in protecting the environment, you do not have to travel to the Amazon or the Antarctic. You can begin at home. In your own community, you can raise public awareness and support Greenpeace in many ways. In fact, young people are helping out every day. Some help support overseas projects. Others volunteer for projects in their home communities. Here are some examples:

Set up a recycling program in your home, community, or school. By making sure to recycle pop cans, bottles, paper, and cardboard, you will be keeping these items from ending up in the landfill. This will help make the earth a cleaner place.

Write a letter to your local newspaper. Writing a letter allows your voice to be heard and will help to educate others at the same time. Greenpeace knows how important it is to get public support and raise environmental awareness.

Become an Ancient Forest Ambassador. These ambassadors represent the interests of ancient forests around the world. Ancient Forest Ambassadors start up campaigns, distribute leaflets, collect signatures, and write articles for school newspapers. They can also carry out "ancient forest inspections" of schools, sports halls, and youth centers, and advise fellow students about school materials that are forest friendly.

To find out more about the role of Ancient Forest Ambassadors, visit the Greenpeace Kids for Forests Web site at www.greenpeace.org/kidsforests/

Where to Write

International	United States	Canada

Greenpeace International
Keizersgracht 176
1016 DW Amsterdam
The Netherlands

The World Conservation Union
Rue Mauverney 28
1196 Gland
Switzerland

For Mother Earth
Maria Hendrikaplein 5
9000 Gent
Belgium

Greenpeace USA
702 H Street NW
Washington, DC 20001

World Wildlife Fund
1250 Twenty-Fourth Street NW
P.O. Box 97180
Washington, DC

Greenpeace Canada
Suite 605,
250 Dundas Street W.
Toronto, ON
M5T 2Z5

The Sierra Club of Canada, National Office
412-1 Nicholas Street
Ottawa, ON
K1N 7B7

The Canadian Nature Federation
Suite 606,
1 Nicholas Street
Ottawa, ON
K1N 7B7

In the Classroom

EXERCISE ONE:

Make Your Own Brochure

Organizations such as Greenpeace use brochures to inform the public about their activities. To make your own Greenpeace brochure, you will need:
- paper
- ruler
- pencil
- color pens or markers

1. Using your ruler as a guide, fold a piece of paper into three equal parts. Your brochure should now have a cover page, a back page, and inside pages.
2. Using your color markers, design a cover page for your brochure. Make sure you include a title.
3. Divide the inside pages into sections. Use the following questions as a guide.
   - What is the organization?
   - How did it get started?
   - Who started it?
   - Who does it help?
4. Using the information found in this book, summarize in point form the key ideas for each topic. Add photographs or illustrations.
5. On the back page, write down the address and contact information for Greenpeace.
6. Photocopy your brochure and give copies to your friends, family, and classmates.

EXERCISE TWO:

Send a Letter to Your Congressperson

To express concern about a particular issue, you can write a letter to your member of congress. This can be an effective way to make the government aware of issues that need its attention. To write a letter, all you need is a pen and paper or a computer.

1. Find out the name and address of your congressperson by contacting your local librarian. You can also search the Internet.
2. Write your name, address, and phone number at the top of the letter.
3. When addressing your letter, use the congressperson's official title.
4. Outline your concerns in the body of the letter. Share any personal experiences you may have that relate to your concerns. Use information found in this book to strengthen your concerns.
5. Request a reply to your letter. This ensures that your letter has been read.
6. Ask your friends and family to write their own letters.

Further Reading

Bohlen, Jim. *Making Waves: The Origin and Future of Greenpeace*. Montreal, Canada: Black Rose Books, 2000.

Brown, Michael and John May. *The Greenpeace Story*. London: DK Publishing, 1991.

Espeland, Pamela, and Barbara A. Lewis. *The Kid's Guide to Service Projects: Over 500 Service Ideas for Young People Who Want to Make a Difference*. Minneapolis: Free Spirit Publishing, 1995.

Pringle, Lawrence and Bobbie Moore (illus.). *Taking Care of the Earth: Kids in Action*. Minneapolis, MN: Econo-Clad Books, 1999.

Pringle, Lawrence. *The Environmental Movement: From Its Roots to the Challenges of a New Century*. New York: HarperCollins Juvenile Books, 2000.

Web Sites

Greenpeace International
www.greenpeace.org
The Web site for Greenpeace International contains information on current Greenpeace campaigns. Visitors can find links to Greenpeace offices worldwide.

Greenpeace USA
www.greenpeaceusa.org
The Web site for Greenpeace USA provides access to information on Greenpeace activities in the United States and around the world. A history section describes the founding of the organization. There is also a page devoted to Greenpeace's fleet of ships.

Greenpeace Kids For Forests
www.greenpeace.org/kidsforforests/
This Web site for children contains information about the earth's ancient forests. It also provides ideas on how to help save the environment.

Glossary

activists: people who believe in action for political purposes

atmosphere: the mixture of gases that surround the earth

biodiversity: a variety of species

boycotts: refusals to deal with organizations or countries, usually to express disapproval

direct action: the use of action, such as strikes and demonstrations, for political purposes

drift nets: large fishing nets, kept upright by weights at the bottom and floats at the top; allowed to drift with the tide

extinction: the death of all living organisms in a species

genes: sequences of proteins in a cell that pass on information

global warming: the increase in temperature of the earth's atmosphere

lobbying: trying to influence members of government

ozone: a layer in the atmosphere that helps control the earth's temperature

pod: a group of whales

Quaker: someone belonging to a Christian movement devoted to peaceful principles

ratified: approved by a country's government

renewable: capable of being replaced by natural ecological cycles

treaties: written agreements between countries

Index